21 Days of Generosity Challenge

Experiencing the Joy That Comes From a Giving Heart

CJ Hitz

CONTENTS

21 Days of Generosity Challenge

When I was a kid growing up in the small logging town of Myrtle Creek, Oregon, I had the opportunity to watch several instances of generosity that have stuck with me ever since. They involved my dad and a homeless man named "Claude."

Claude would roam the highways and byways on his worn out bicycle and a huge pack with all of his earthly belongings. I am still amazed at how the man was able to pedal his bike with that load on his back!

On many occasions, while accompanying my dad as he drove into town, we would see Claude riding on the side of the road. Typically, dad would pull ahead and stop alongside the road to wait for Claude. It was about this time that I would shrink into my seat for fear of being noticed by any of my friends.

To be honest, I was embarrassed to be seen with this "hobo" of a guy who had the odor of someone who had not taken a shower in years. My friends and I had nicknames for many of the "colorful characters" wandering our area. Claude was simply known as "Dirt Claude" – as in a clump of dirt.

But my dad saw through the dirt. He saw a man who still deserved to be treated with dignity and respect, regardless of the circumstances that led to his homelessness. As Claude would ride up next to our truck, dad would actually step out and greet him. I can still see Claude's big toothless smile as he would say, "Hey Kenny, good to see you."

They would chat for 15-20 minutes before dad would almost always put a $20 bill in Claude's hand and give him a hug upon saying goodbye. Neither of them ever seemed in a rush. Claude would soak up the attention that every human being craves and my dad was more than willing to offer. It was generosity that went beyond just money.

One day my dad came home with some sad news. "Claude died yesterday." My heart sank as I thought about how often people made fun of Claude, myself included. "Apparently, they found Claude frozen to death under an overpass…said his body was as hard as an ice cube."

As hard as an ice cube.

Those words still ring in my ears to this day. What a lonely, agonizing way to spend your last hours on this earth. Claude could not have been older than 30. It very well could be that my dad was the last kind face Claude ever saw before his passing.

After all these years, my dad's actions remain a powerful and vivid example of rich generosity not easily found in our world. It is the kind of generosity that Jesus demonstrated daily during the 33 years he walked on this earth.

It is an example worth following.

Over the years, the Lord has given me many opportunities to show generosity. Unfortunately, I have not responded to all of those opportunities. In fact, only heaven knows the full impact of what I have missed out on and what others were deprived of as a result.

Over the course of these next 21 days, it is my hope to grow deeper as I'm challenged to be more generous with my money, time, talents and, finally, my love for God and others. It is a chance to allow the Lord to sharpen my "generosity senses" and be more tuned into His frequency.

Regarding Jesus, I recently heard a child say, "He's the man that gave God a good reputation." Ha! So true! Let's look at these next 21 days as a jumpstart that leads to a lifestyle of generosity that gives God a good reputation!

Will You Join Me?

What about you? Will you consider joining me in these 21 Days of Generosity Challenge? It may look different for you and that is okay. Simply ask God what He wants you to do and then do it.

CJ

DAY 1

Shelley and I met Jason when we first began attending a church in Findlay, Ohio back in April 2005. To say he is a very needy young man would be a huge understatement. Jason is the type of person who started off with two strikes against him from the time he was born. His dad died when he was 5 years old and a year later he and his sisters were put into foster care after their mom struggled to provide for their needs.

Now in his mid-twenties, Jason still has a severe speech impediment which makes it difficult to understand what he is saying. This alone tends to repel people from him. He is the kind of person no employer would ever think of hiring.

He recently spent two months in jail for stealing his roommate's credit card. He has been hooked on drugs & alcohol throughout his life and has faithfully attended Alcoholics Anonymous until he was kicked out for being so annoying.

His 6'0" and 115 pound frame makes him look malnourished. Several times, I have had the opportunity to hang out with Jason and buy him a meal. On most of these occasions, I will tell him to order anything he wants. Without fail, he orders the most expensive item on the menu!

Watching Jason dig into that food is a sight to behold. It feels good knowing I am helping put a couple pounds on his gaunt body.

Shelley and I now live in Colorado Springs, Colorado where we are 1,300 miles from Jason. Needless to say, phone calls are the best we can do. This leads me to today's generosity challenge.

I need to call Jason and give him some of my time and attention. I know he has been craving it because he called me 31 times in January. I am ashamed to say I either missed or did not answer any of his calls. As I mentioned previously, Jason can be a bit needy. But aren't we all at times?

So I called Jason and we talked for about 20 minutes. He read me some of the songs he has been writing. He also told me he came close to taking his own life a little over a year ago. "What do you think prevented you from doing it?" I asked. "I think God did," he responded.

I closed the call by praying for Jason and thanking the Lord for keeping Jason alive. He is on this earth for a purpose and he matters to his Creator.

Could it be that God has placed me in Jason's life to help remind him of that truth?

"As far as I am concerned, the greatest suffering is to feel alone, unwanted, unloved. The greatest suffering is also having no one, forgetting what an intimate, truly human relationship is, not knowing what it means to be loved, not having a family or friends." Mother Teresa

"We loved you so much that we shared with you not only God's Good News but our own lives, too." 1 Thessalonians 2:8

Application:

- Think of that person in your life who can be annoying or overly needy. This could be a friend or family member. For some reason, God has placed you in their lives for a reason. Even though there are times you would prefer to just sweep them under the rug, you cannot seem to shake them. Go pick them up and hang out with them for an hour. And let them pick whatever they want on the menu. :)

DAY 2

Over the past few years, many families have suffered financial hardship due to an economy that has been hit hard. Rising unemployment rates, job layoffs and foreclosures have all taken their toll.

Recently, we had the opportunity to help a family that has been struggling to stay afloat financially. The Lord provided some extra funds for us that were totally unexpected and we were able to bless this family with a $100 Wal-Mart gift card.

Here's a thank-you note we received from the wife/mom…

"Ok…I received the envelope in the mail today!!! Thank you…so very much…what a tremendous blessing…I'm actually out of words…which as you know for me doesn't happen often!!!"

What an incredible feeling to be used by the Lord to meet the needs of others.

"You have not lived today until you have done something for someone who can never repay you." John Bunyan

"The LORD had said to Abram, 'Leave your native country, your relatives, and your father's family, and go to the land that I will show you. I will make you into a great nation. I will bless you and make you famous, and you will be a blessing to others.'" Genesis 12:1-2

Application:

- Is there a family you know who has been struggling financially? Perhaps you have been blessed with some unexpected funds in order to bless that family. Put some money (any amount) or a gift card in the mail along with a note of encouragement to that family. Let them know you are praying for them as well.

DAY 3

For some people, the gift of time can be more valuable than any amount of money. For example, we know a family that is doing well financially because the husband works as a vice president for a company and his wife works full-time as well. With two children ages 3 and 2, the wife/mom has her hands full with little time for a break.

Shelley recently decided to bless them by coming over to watch the kids to allow her friend the time needed to run some much needed errands. Not having children of our own yet, this also allowed Shelley to get her "kid fix" for a few hours.

The family really appreciated this kind of generosity which we will be happy to offer again in the future.

"For it is in giving that we receive." St. Francis of Assisi

"So let's not get tired of doing what is good. At just the right time we will reap a harvest of blessing if we don't give up. Therefore, whenever we have the opportunity, we should do good to everyone—especially to those in the family of faith." Galatians 6:9-10

Application:

- Think of a family you could bless by babysitting their kids. Another idea is to offer to clean someone's house, which is another way to bless them with the gift of your time.

DAY 4

One of the saddest attempts at "generosity" I have ever heard is when a missionary friend of ours in Belize told us the following story. He said he knew missionaries in India that would receive used tea bags as donations. Their supporters assured them that the tea bags had "only been used once."

However well-meaning these folks might have been, it goes to show how Christians can sometimes give away shoddy stuff in the name of being generous. Unfortunately, when I did a little more research, I found that missionaries in many other countries had also received used tea bags as gifts.

I admit I have been guilty of being a cheapskate on numerous occasions throughout my life. On one of these occasions I stuffed a bag full of old, ragged t-shirts that I would bring with me on a missions trip in order to "bless" those poor people with something American.

I heard another pathetic example regarding the shoe boxes filled with toys and school supplies that some ministries collect and ship overseas to needy children. Apparently, some families have filled these boxes with used junk they no longer want themselves. A booklet sharing the love of Jesus Christ is then placed inside each box.

What message are we sending?

"I ask one thing: do not tire of giving, but do not give your leftovers. Give until it hurts, until you feel the pain." Mother Teresa
"Do to others as you would like them to do to you." Luke 6:31

Application:

- There is certainly nothing wrong with bringing our used clothing and other items to places like Goodwill and the Salvation Army who will then find people who truly need those things. Sometimes, Shelley & I are those people in need!

- The next opportunity you have to bless someone in need such as a missionary overseas, filling a shoe box with toys or giving a coat or pair of shoes to a homeless person; I encourage you to give something of sacrifice...something that you would love to have yourself (i.e. name brand clothing, Nike shoes, good quality food).

DAY 5

In the New Testament the word kairos means "the appointed time in the purpose of God," the time when God acts (i.e. Mark 1:15, the kairos is fulfilled).

Years ago, I heard about a prison ministry called Kairos where volunteers serve as God's instrument through which His love, grace and mercy are expressed to the participants in a real and profound way. These Kairos weekends are famous for the thousands of chocolate chip cookies that are baked and donated for the purpose of blessing prison participants. It is not uncommon for inmates to begin crying when they are given a couple dozen of these cookies.

I have yet to meet a person who does not like chocolate chip cookies. I have met a few who are not able to eat them due to diabetes, but all of those folks wish they could.

A couple years ago at Christmas time, we decided to bless several households up and down our street with a dozen of the most delicious cookies made by a popular local bakery. We also included a note about God's love inside each box.

It was amazing to see all the looks that people gave us as if to say, "Are you for real?" Some of the families invited us inside their home and a few put sincere thank-you notes in the mail.

All of them smiled when they opened the boxes. :)

"Do all the good you can, By all the means you can,
In all the ways you can, In all the places you can,
At all the times you can, To all the people you can,
As long as ever you can." John Wesley

"I was naked, and you gave me clothing. I was sick, and you cared for me. I was in prison, and you visited me." Matthew 25:36

Application:

- Visit the website of Kairos Prison Ministry International (www.kairosprisonministry.org) to find out how you can serve a prison near you. If you cannot be part of a volunteer team that goes inside a prison, be a volunteer chocolate chip cookie baker!

- Make it a goal to bake a dozen chocolate chip cookies for every household on your street at some point. Include an encouraging note with scripture for each family. This is a great way to meet your neighbors. After writing down the names of each house you visit, commit to praying for each household on a regular basis.

DAY 6

A couple of years ago Shelley and I decided to simplify and get rid of a bunch of our belongings by having a garage sale. Anything we did not sell we donated to our nearest Salvation Army. It felt so good to "clean house" and learn to live with less clutter.

To be honest, part of the reason for simplifying was out of necessity in order to live out of a 125 square foot Toyota RV. We simply had to pick and choose what we could take aboard the RV.

Although the RV lifestyle did not work out like we had planned (we ended up selling it), we still learned the value of living life with few possessions. It can be a freeing thing to get rid of things we do not really need.

"May God give you - and me - the courage, the wisdom, the strength always to hold the kingdom of God as the number one priority of our lives. To do so, is to live in simplicity" Richard Foster

"They sold their property and possessions and shared the money with those in need." Acts 2:45

Application:

- As a family, go through your whole house and decide which possessions you no longer need and can live without. Remember, this is not an excuse to go shopping to replace those items. Part of the lesson is learning to live in simplicity.

- Pick a day to have a garage/yard sale and donate all the proceeds to a ministry that specifically helps the poor. Examples might include your local city mission or relief organizations like World Vision. Anything that does not sell goes to your nearest Salvation Army or Goodwill.

- Another way to use the proceeds from your garage/ yard sale is to find and befriend some homeless people in your area and buy meals, clothing and hygiene items for them. By sitting down and having a meal with them, you are able to show them dignity as human beings and give the Lord an opening to touch their lives.

DAY 7

I have a friend who makes it a regular practice of paying the toll for one or two cars behind him and leaving a gospel tract or encouraging note for the toll booth attendant to hand to those folks. It is always fun to watch their reactions in his rearview mirror. Some of these people have been known to speed up in order to pull alongside and thank him with a "thumbs up" signal.

Oh how I wish I could have been a recipient on a couple occasions when I had no toll money and received the bill in the mail!

"We can do no great things; only small things with great love." Mother Teresa

"In the same way, let your good deeds shine out for all to see, so that everyone will praise your heavenly Father." Matthew 5:16

Application:

- Arm yourself with some extra change that you set aside for toll booth goodwill. Depending on where you live, toll rates can vary. Whether it is fifty cents or five dollars, this little act of generosity can go a long way in making someone's day.

- Write out some encouraging notes for the toll booth attendant to hand to drivers behind you. An example might be...

"Because God has been so good to me, I am able to bless you today!"

DAY 8

One of the most touching acts of generosity I have seen firsthand is when my wife Shelley made the decision to donate her wedding ring to a ministry called Gospel For Asia.

This ministry started by K.P. Yohannon is on the frontlines of reaching some of the most unreached people on the planet with the gospel. They do this primarily by training up native missionaries who are able to live on less than $1500 per year compared to the average western missionary family who needs an average of $50,000 or more per year.

These native missionaries already know the language and culture which allows them to immediately begin sharing the life-changing message of Christ with those who have never heard.

Needless to say, we were deeply touched as we heard stories of how the Lord was using these humble servants in some of the most hostile conditions. As we thought about how Shelley's ring could support two native missionaries for a year, she felt the Lord tugging on her heart.

"Are you sure you want to do this?" I asked.

"I'm sure", she replied. She continued, "When I think of the eternal impact that could be made in exchange for this diamond, it is not a difficult decision."

And with the decision made, we mailed the ring to Gospel For Asia the next day. We look forward to seeing its full impact when we reach heaven.

"He is no fool who gives what he cannot keep to gain that which he cannot lose." Jim Elliot

"Jesus told him, "If you want to be perfect, go and sell all your possessions and give the money to the poor, and you will have treasure in heaven. Then come, follow me." Matthew 19:21

Application:

- This is a heavier day in the challenge. We are not asking everyone to go out and donate their wedding rings like Shelley did. However, maybe the Lord is tugging on your heart in a similar way.

- Do you have something of value that you know could be used to help expand the Kingdom of God? Perhaps a piece of jewelry, a valuable baseball card or another collectible that is simply collecting dust? Ask the Lord to show you specifically how you can be generous in this way.

DAY 9

When I was 14 years old, the church I was raised in got a new pastor. John Gustafson and his family had been in Portland before moving to our little logging town of three thousand people in southern Oregon.

When I think of the word "faithfulness" I think of Pastor John. It has now been over 25 years since he took over as shepherd of Tri City Baptist Church. From visiting elderly shut-ins to taking the youth group on numerous excursions, this gentle and humble man gave himself completely to the community.

In the spring of 1993, I submitted my life to Jesus while attending Anderson University in Indiana. Upon my return home that summer to work in a local lumber mill, Pastor John took me under his guidance in order to mentor me and help me grow in my relationship with the Lord.

I have fond memories of us hopping into the church van and heading over to the Feed Lot restaurant for lunch. I always looked forward to these times as a new believer where I would soak in Pastor John's wisdom and insight. At 19 going on 20, I was a young man trying to gain my footing and the Lord provided someone to look up to in the process.

As I write this, Pastor John is dying. The cancer has taken its toll on his body and he is now in his last days, yet still pastoring from his bed and by telephone. This man who has given so much of himself is about ready to receive his eternal reward.

Thank you for your generous example in my life Pastor John. I am so grateful the Lord touched my life through you.

[Update] Pastor John Gustafson went to be with the Lord on March 1st 2013. He was a true warrior for Christ.

"Only one life, 'twill soon be past,
Only what's done for Christ will last.
And when I am dying, how happy I'll be,
If the lamp of my life has been burned out for Thee."
C.T. Studd

"Precious in the sight of the LORD is the death of his faithful servants." Psalm 116:15

Application:

- Is there someone in your life who might benefit from you generously pouring yourself into them for a season? Think of some possibilities and ask the Lord for discernment.

- Think of someone who had a profound impact in your life and write them a letter of thanks and gratitude. This could be a former mentor, teacher or pastor who God generously used to aid in your maturity.

DAY 10

I love running. Since taking it up again in the Spring of 2008, it has become my favorite hobby and form of exercise. To be honest, running can be a very selfish endeavor as we seek to set goals, train to achieve those goals, and finally accomplish what we set out to do. I have devoted countless hours to tap into my running potential. I have also spent thousands of dollars on shoes, gear, race fees and travel to races across the country.

Don't get me wrong, there have also been many benefits to this simple sport of putting one foot in front of the other like making lots of new friends, losing over fifty pounds, increased energy levels and running for some pretty neat causes.

I ran a 5k race a couple years ago that was organized by parents who lost their 10 year-old daughter to cancer. Proceeds from the race go toward providing scholarships to her fellow classmates upon their graduation in 2013. Those classmates just graduated and it looks like the race will continue on.

In another race, I had the opportunity to run on behalf of Living Water International, an organization that helps provide clean drinking water to impoverished countries around the world. They provided a racing shirt and a personal webpage where folks could donate toward my campaign goal. All proceeds went to help bring something that so many of us take for granted each day – clean, clear, pure drinking water.

I guess you could say it was a "refreshing" way to be the hands and feet of Jesus, who the bible refers to as the Living Water.

"God made me fast. And when I run, I feel His pleasure." Eric Liddell – 1924 Olympic gold medalist

"For physical training is of some value, but godliness has value for all things, holding promise for both the present life and the life to come." I Timothy 4:8

Application:

- Though you may not be a runner, is there a hobby or sport you could use to bless others?

- If you are interested in running a race (any distance) for Team Living Water, visit www.Water.cc for more information on how to do so. It is a fantastic organization.

- Consider organizing your own local 5k road or trail race for the purpose of raising funds for a life-changing cause.

DAY 11

Recently, I heard a sad story about a pastor and a waitress that lit up the social media circuits. When the pastor received the bill with an automatic tip of 18% included (for groups of 8 or more), they decided to cross out the tip line and leave a big fat "0" instead. Along with that, the pastor wrote the following note...

"I give God 10 percent. Why do you get 18?"

The waitress then decided to post the receipt on Reddit where it spread like wildfire. As a result, this pastor called the restaurant and demanded that this waitress be fired due to the embarrassment it caused him. She was fired the next day.

I cringe when I hear stories like that, especially when it involves a Christian leader. As followers of the most generous man in history, Jesus, we should be the most generous people on the planet.

The next time I go into a restaurant, I plan to leave a generous tip along with writing the following note...

"It is more blessed to give than to receive." – Jesus

As followers of Christ, let's do our best to make Him look good to those who are watching.

"I like your Christ, I do not like your Christians. Your Christians are so unlike your Christ." Mahatma Gandhi

"In the same way, let your light shine before others, that they may see your good deeds and glorify your Father in heaven." Matthew 5:16

Application:

- The next time you go into a sit down restaurant, make it a point to leave a generous tip along with an encouraging note thanking them for their service. Waiters and waitresses rely on tips since their base pay is way below minimum wage.

DAY 12

On Saturday June 23rd 2012, the Waldo Canyon fire broke out on the far west side of Colorado Springs. Within two weeks, over 350 homes would be claimed in its path of destruction. Shelley and I had to evacuate for two days after the fire came within two miles of where we live. Thanks to the tireless efforts of hundreds of brave firefighters and volunteers, the fire was eventually contained and extinguished.

At the time, the Waldo Canyon fire became the costliest wildfire in Colorado history. Little did we know that it would be surpassed almost a year later by the Black Forest fire which erupted on Tuesday June 11th 2013. Full containment of this fire would come nine days later but not before over 509 homes were lost.

It was stunning to see the level of generosity exhibited by people all over this hard hit city. As the mandatory evacuations hit over 40,000 people, donations came streaming in. In the first 24 hours, over 102,000 pounds of food had been donated. That's 51 tons!

Schools and churches opened their buildings, people opened their homes and wallets, and a community was strengthened once again through trial.

Oh…and our gracious God brought some much needed rain.

"It is no use walking anywhere to preach unless our walking is our preaching." Francis of Assisi

"You will be enriched in every way so that you can be generous on every occasion, and through us your generosity will result in thanksgiving to God." 2 Corinthians 9:11

Application:

- Let's face it, natural disasters can strike at any time and at any place. From earthquakes to tornadoes, hurricanes, fires, floods and volcanic eruptions, none of us is immune regardless of where we call home. Perhaps you have recently experienced one in your own neck of the woods.

- The next time you hear about a natural disaster on the news, consider making a sacrificial donation of some kind to help those who are suffering. This could be in the form of volunteering your time, donating cash or buying sacks of groceries for a family reeling after a disaster. If it is a disaster in another country, find out which organizations are receiving donations for relief. One such organization to consider is World Vision – SamaritansPurse.org

DAY 13

In the past few weeks, a few of our friends have enjoyed the blessing of delivering babies into this world. One family already had two young children and the other two families had three. Needless to say, this makes for a tiring adjustment for the parents in these first few weeks of the newborn's life.

We had the privilege of bringing meals to each family in order to ease their burden. Shelley received rave reviews for her signature vegetable lasagna dish. One of the families has an 11 year-old who is known to be a very picky eater, but said they devoured this "healthy" meal – an added bonus!

It seems like such a small thing, but each of these families were very grateful. It feels good to help out in these small ways.

"We make a living by what we get, we make a life by what we give." Sir Winston Churchill

"All the believers were one in heart and mind. No one claimed that any of their possessions was their own, but they shared everything they had." Acts 4:32

Application:

- Think of a family you know who might be in need, whether they've just had a baby or perhaps are going through a medical crisis. Consider bringing them a meal (or meals) to help during this time in their lives.

DAY 14

If you have been to Wal-Mart recently, you have no doubt seen a wide variety of people. It is not difficult to spot people who are in need - financially, emotionally, socially and spiritually.

So many times I walk into our local Wal-Mart with the intent to get in and get out as quickly as possible without really noticing or paying attention to those around me. Not so with Jesus...

"When Jesus landed and saw a large crowd, <u>he had compassion on them</u>, because they were like sheep without a shepherd." *(Mark 6:34)*

"During those days another large crowd gathered. Since they had nothing to eat, Jesus called his disciples to him and said, <u>"I have compassion for these people</u>; they have already been with me three days and have nothing to eat." (Mark 8:1-2)

Jesus was extremely generous and compassionate wherever he went. He noticed people. As we spend time with Him, I am pretty sure some of that will rub off on us as well.

"If you can't feed a hundred people, then feed just one."
Mother Teresa

"Whoever is kind to the poor lends to the LORD, and he will reward them for what they have done." Proverbs 19:17

Application:

- The next time you are in Wal-Mart (or maybe a grocery store), go there with the intention of blessing someone in need at the checkout counter by paying their bill. Trust me, you can do this without looking like a stalker. Perhaps it is a mom with children buying groceries or a man who looks like he is homeless or of lower means.

- Before walking into the store, pray for the Lord to lead you to someone He has in mind. Also, be prepared for the person to be blown away and possibly break down in tears at this kind of generosity.

DAY 15

A few years ago, my father-in-law had to spend several weeks in a nursing home in order to recover from a traumatic brain injury he sustained.

I have all the respect in the world for nursing home employees. Day after day they have to perform tasks that few of us ever want to sign up for. We saw this firsthand whenever we came to visit Shelley's dad.

This was not our first time visiting a nursing home. For several years, it was a family tradition to sing Christmas carols to the residents on Christmas Eve. These folks just soaked up the time we spent with them and were genuinely thankful for our visit.

Nursing homes are full of so many lonely people in need of a friend who shows them love and attention. Many people have simply been abandoned there by family members.

We also have a lot we can learn from someone who has lived 70+ years if we will just give them a listening ear. Sure, many of these people have deteriorated mentally, but we have encountered many who are still very clear and sharp in their thinking.

I think it is time to schedule my next visit and bring a bag of love and joy to share.

"We are all so much together, but we are all dying of loneliness." Albert Schweitzer

"The King will reply, 'Truly I tell you, whatever you did for one of the least of these brothers and sisters of mine, you did for me.' Matthew 25:40

Application:

- Look for the nearest nursing home in your area and call to let them know you are interested in visiting residents there. Some require visitors to fill out forms and some allow you to walk in with little or no red tape.

- After this initial visit, you may find that you would like to visit once a week, every other week or once a month. No matter what, you are sure to find it a rewarding way to show generosity.

DAY 16

As a runner, I've been thinking more about how my running can make an impact on others. As I mentioned on Day 10, running by itself can be a selfish endeavor.

Recently, I ran across (no pun intended) a cool organization called Back On My Feet (www. BackOnMyFeet.org). In 2007, Founder Anne Mahlum was looking for purpose. Living in Philadelphia, she would regularly encounter homeless men when she ran by the Sunday Breakfast Rescue Mission. She realized she could help these people if she stopped running by them and started running with them.

Today, Back On My Feet has 14 chapters across the nation using running to help the homeless. I really do encourage you to check out their program.

I guess you might call it "putting feet to our faith!"

"You only ever grow as a human being if you're outside your comfort zone." Percy Cerutty

"How beautiful on the mountains are the feet of those who bring good news, who proclaim peace, who bring good tidings, who proclaim salvation, who say to Zion, 'Your God reigns!'" Isaiah 52:7

Application:

- Again, you may not be a runner but perhaps you have another talent God can use to help bridge the gap to those in need. If so, contact your nearest rescue mission or shelter and present your idea (i.e. golf, biking, bowling, flag football, sewing, etc.)

- Contact local businesses to see if they would be willing to donate equipment required for the activity you will be doing with these men or women. As for me, I'll be seeking donations of running shoes and apparel to give to the men I'll be running with.

DAY 17

"Do you have any spare change?"

Many of us have been approached at some point in our lives by someone who asked us this question. It may even be followed up with "anything helps."

It is amazing how quickly our spare change consisting of quarters, dimes, nickels and pennies can add up over time. Some of us keep our spare change in the middle console of our car. Others throw it in a drawer, plastic baggie or piggy bank.

Sometimes, spare change falls out of our pockets between couch cushions. Since I am one of those people who puts my spare change in the middle console of my car, I inevitably lose coins that fall under the two front seats. There have been times in the past when I have cleaned out the car only to find a treasure trove!

Putting our spare change to good use is another way to demonstrate generosity. What if those coins could help create a business that helps lift someone out of poverty?

Hope International (www.HopeInternational.org) is an organization that offers small business loans and the hope of the Gospel message to people caught in a cycle of poverty. They currently work in 16 countries in South America, Africa, Eastern Europe and Asia.

When your loose change adds up to at least $50, you can help provide a micro loan to a family in need.

Now that's "change" we can all believe in!

"A business that makes nothing but money is a poor business." Henry Ford

"Or suppose a woman has ten silver coins and loses one. Doesn't she light a lamp, sweep the house and search carefully until she finds it? And when she finds it, she calls her friends and neighbors together and says, 'Rejoice with me; I have found my lost coin.'" Luke 15:8-9

Application:

• Come together as a family to discuss collecting spare change for the purpose of being generous and using it to bless others in need. Hope International is just one example of an organization that can squeeze the most good out of your coins.

DAY 18

"Nature's Nectar" is one way to describe it.

I absolutely love a good 'cuppa joe!' Even a non-coffee drinker will agree that coffee has to be one of the most intoxicating aromas on planet earth.

One of the "perks" for me is actually going into different coffee houses and enjoying the peaceful ambience. If I could afford it, I would travel to every state in search of the best coffee houses and write a book about it!

A small act of generosity that has been a joy is buying the coffee for either the person ahead of me or behind me (or both). Even though it usually comes to less than $5, people are both shocked and grateful to be recipients. If they ask me why I am doing it, I like to respond with something along the lines of, "I'm just passing along some of what God has given me."

This is such a small (yet tasty) way to make God look good in the eyes of others. God is indeed good to us as evidenced by all the little gifts He lavishes on us. Coffee being one of them.

On that note, it is now time for my "afternoon injection."

"Coffee is a language in itself." Jackie Chan

"Truly I tell you, anyone who gives you a cup of water in my name because you belong to the Messiah will certainly not lose their reward." Mark 9:41

Application:

• The next time you visit a coffee house, pick up the tab for the person in front of you or behind you. If you don't visit coffee houses, how about doing the same thing at an ice cream or frozen yogurt shop? Either way, you will get the same fun reaction.

Some of my favorite coffee houses I've had the privilege of visiting over the years...

- Urban Steam – www.UrbanSteamCoffee.com
- R&R Coffee Café – www.RnRCoffeeCafe.com
- The Conservatory – www.ConservatoryCoffeeAndTea.com
- Café Julia – www.CafeJulia.com
- Indian Shores Coffee Company – 19221 Gulf Blvd. Indian Shores, FL 33785

- George House Coffee & Tea Co. – 1041 N. Main St. Findlay, OH 45840
- Higher Ground Coffee Shop – 230 NC St. Pine Ridge, SD 57770
- Clint's Bakery & Coffee House – www. ClintsBakery.com

DAY 19

As a follower of Jesus, I cannot think of a more powerful, effective use of my time than to pray. Unfortunately, I don't always live my life as if I truly believe this.

It is so easy to get distracted by trivial things and forget about prayer altogether. We live in a world where people scurry around and fill every hour of the day with all kinds of busy-ness.

I like to refer to prayer as "talkin' with Daddy." And that's really what it is when we simplify it. It blesses God's heart when we come to him on our own without being prodded. If you are a parent, think about how happy you feel when your little son or daughter wants to come sit on your lap and show you affection... without being asked.

Spending time in prayer is an act of generosity toward God but also a way we can be generous in our time toward others. When we pray for others, we are saying, "You matter to me." Lifting others up to our Papa in heaven is another way of agreeing with Him that they have extremely high value.

Prayer is the proof that we're relying on God. And it is a powerful demonstration of generosity!

"To be a Christian without prayer is no more possible than to be alive without breathing." Martin Luther

"I urge, then, first of all, that petitions, prayers, intercession and thanksgiving be made for all people— for kings and all those in authority, that we may live peaceful and quiet lives in all godliness and holiness. This is good, and pleases God our Savior, who wants all people to be saved and to come to a knowledge of the truth." 1 Timothy 2:1-4

Application:

- Take time to write out a list of people you can spend time praying for on a regular basis. Feel free to ask these folks how you can specifically be praying for them. They will be so grateful you are thinking of them in this way.

- As you spend time in prayer, make it a regular practice of thanking and praising God for the countless ways He has shown so much generosity toward you.

- Finally, consider getting a notebook or journal in order to write down the ways you see the Lord answering prayer in the lives of those you are praying for.

DAY 20

Looking for a fun group activity? How about a free car wash? A couple years ago, Shelley and I were speaking at a school in Richmond, Virginia. On one of the days, we were able to take part in a car wash the middle school students were doing as an act of generosity for staff, parents and anyone else who wanted to stop in for a freebie.

It was a great bonding time with the students and staff serving and also a fun way to show generosity. Who doesn't feel good after getting their car washed?

Soap, sunshine, spray and a smile…all free of charge!

"A little thought and a little kindness are often worth more than a great deal of money." John Ruskin

"Have mercy on me, O God, according to your unfailing love; according to your great compassion blot out my transgressions.

Wash away all my iniquity and cleanse me from my sin." Psalm 51: 1-2

Application:

- Gather a group of people together willing to take part in a free community car wash. Then pick out a location like a school, church or shopping center. Have each person or family bring towels, wash rags, brushes and soap.

- For some added encouragement, you could even give each car wash recipient some candy along with a kind note. An example could be, "Thanks for stopping in and allowing us to serve you by washing your car. God bless you!" You could then include a scripture like the one above.

DAY 21

Last week I had the opportunity to travel with some buddies to a 5k race we ran in Evergreen, Colorado. One of the guys has a minivan we all loaded into for the hour and a half trip. We called it a "manventure!"

After the race we took a different route back home in order to stop at a great roadside restaurant to celebrate and enjoy a more scenic drive. The food was delicious and the conversation enjoyable. Soon enough the waitress brought the bill which was on one ticket. I thought to myself, "I will go ahead and pay it with my debit card and the others can just pay me back what they owe."

But then I sensed an inner voice say, "Don't ask them to pay you back, just bless them." It took me a few seconds to finally accept this since I knew our bank account was not exactly overflowing. Or was it?

After all, if I put my complete trust in God, He is my Provider. He is the supplier of my bank account and His provision is limitless. It is nothing for Him to reimburse me in other ways for choosing to be generous.

And when it comes down to it, generosity really is a choice. Each day presents another opportunity to be generous with the time, talents and financial resources God has blessed us with. These daily choices eventually add up to a lifestyle.

It is so liberating to have an open hand in giving. It is what we were made for. Conversely, it is draining and tiresome to walk through life with hands that are clinched tightly to stuff.

By the way, my buddies were blown away by me paying that restaurant bill last week. To be honest, so was I! But then again, that's simply the nature of the God I serve.

I am so thankful for the example Jesus gave us as He embodied a life of generosity. Will you join me as we strive to follow that example?

"No one has ever become poor by giving." Anne Frank

"The Lord will guide you always; he will satisfy your needs in a sun-scorched land and will strengthen your frame. You will be like a well-watered garden, like a spring whose waters never fail." Isaiah 58:11

Application:

- I challenge you to see if you can "out-give" God today. In other words, go beyond what is comfortable and see if God doesn't bless your life over and over again.

- What will you do on Day 22? Use your creativity to make generosity a lifestyle.

- Begin keeping a "generosity journal" of all the ways God leads you to be generous with your time, talents and financial resources. Also write down those times where you are the recipient of someone else's generosity. As you allow God to lead, you will be amazed at how quickly you can fill up a journal.

CJ AND SHELLEY HITZ

CJ Hitz and his wife, Shelley, enjoy sharing God's Truth through their speaking engagements and their writing. They enjoy spending time outdoors running, hiking, and exploring God's beautiful creation. CJ and Shelley reside in Colorado Springs, Colorado.

To find out more about CJ and to contact him about speaking at your next event in person or online, send an email to cj@cjhitz.com or find him at www.bodyandsoulpublishing.com/about-cj-hitz.

Note from the Author: Reviews are gold to authors! If you have enjoyed this book, would you consider reviewing it on Amazon.com? Thank you!